Suspects

Characters

Ahmed — likes to figure things out

Yasmin — works hard and often comes top

Lewis — doesn't always play by the rules

Myles — likes to make people laugh

Erin and Naomi — always together and up to something

Why do bees hum?

Because they can't remember the words!

In a classroom, the door slams shut.

Lewis: We're all here for the same thing, then?

Ahmed: The test paper has gone missing.

Naomi: And Mr Boyle thinks it was one of us who took it.

Find a Way out

Plays by
Catherine MacPhail

Illustrated by
Amerigo Pinelli

Suspects 3
Lost 18

Published by Pearson Education Limited, Edinburgh Gate, Harlow, Essex, CM20 2JE.

www.pearsonschools.co.uk

Text © Catherine MacPhail 2013

Designed by Georgia Styring
Original illustrations © Pearson Education Limited 2013
Illustrated by Amerigo Pinelli, Advocate-Art Agency

The right of Catherine MacPhail to be identified as author of this work has been asserted by her in accordance with the Copyright, Designs and Patents Act 1988.

First published 2013

17 16 15 14 13
10 9 8 7 6 5 4 3 2 1

British Library Cataloguing in Publication Data
A catalogue record for this book is available from the British Library

ISBN 978 0 435 14423 4

Printed and bound in the UK by Ashford Colour Press.

Acknowledgements
We would like to thank Bangor Central Integrated Primary School, Northern Ireland; Bishop Henderson Church of England Primary School, Somerset; Bletchingdon Parochial Church of England Primary School, Oxfordshire; Brookside Community Primary School, Somerset; Bude Park Primary School, Hull; Carisbrooke Church of England Primary School, Isle of Wight; Cheddington Combined School, Buckinghamshire; Dair House Independent School, Buckinghamshire; Deal Parochial School, Kent; Glebe Infant School, Gloucestershire; Henley Green Primary School, Coventry; Lovelace Primary School, Surrey; Our Lady of Peace Junior School, Slough; Tackley Church of England Primary School, Oxfordshire; and Twyford Church of England School, Buckinghamshire for their invaluable help in the development and trialling of the Bug Club resources.

Every effort has been made to contact copyright holders of material reproduced in this book. Any omissions will be rectified in subsequent printings if notice is given to the publishers.

Myles: Well, I suppose it must have been one of us. The paper went missing during break time, didn't it?

Erin: Yes, and the rest of the class was in the hall, rehearsing for the school concert.

Naomi: We're the only six who aren't in the choir.

Why do bees hum?
Because they can't remember the words!

Myles: I'm not surprised you're not in the choir, Naomi. I've heard your singing.

Naomi: Very funny, Myles.

Yasmin: Well, it wasn't me who stole the paper. I don't have to steal test papers.

Ahmed: Yes, Yasmin always comes top in everything.

Lewis: Well, if I'm a suspect, so is she!

Ahmed: Mr Boyle said he'd be back in half an hour, and then he wanted to hear who did it.

Erin: Well, it wasn't me or Naomi.

Naomi: No, we never do anything wrong. Do we, Erin?

Myles: So why does Mr Boyle call you "The Terrible Two"?

Lewis: Because they're always up to something.

Ahmed: They're always dropping litter in the corridor.

Yasmin: They never do their homework.

Erin: But we never steal things. Do we, Naomi? And certainly not test papers.

Naomi: We never pass tests, anyway.

Yasmin: We all know that.

Myles: So why were you in the classroom during break time?

Erin: Well ... actually ...

Naomi: We were only here because we were freezing in the playground.

Lewis: No wonder you were freezing. You never wear your jackets.

Erin: Us? Wear school jackets?

Naomi: They are **so** not cool!

Myles laughs.

Myles: But they **are** warm.

Ahmed: That's a very weak story.

Erin: Oh, listen to Sherlock Holmes.

Ahmed: I've got it!

Myles: The test paper?

Ahmed: No! We can find out who the culprit is ourselves!

Erin: And when Mr Boyle comes back ...

Naomi: We'll hand him over.

Lewis: What do you mean, "him"?
It could be a **her**.

Yasmin looks at Lewis.

Yasmin: I think we all know who did it.

Lewis: And that would be me, of course?
I get the blame for everything.

Myles: Who put itching powder in
Mr Boyle's PE shorts?

Lewis: That would have been me.

Ahmed: And who put glue on the
handlebars of the caretaker's bike?

Lewis: Just a bit of fun.

Naomi: Great. Mystery solved. It was Lewis.

Erin: Yes, let's go!

Lewis: Wait a minute! It wasn't me.

Ahmed: So you're pleading not guilty, then?

Lewis: I'm not pleading anything.
Anyway, why were **you** in the
classroom, Ahmed?

Myles: No mystery there. Ahmed is always tidying up.

Ahmed: You all leave a terrible mess in this classroom.

Naomi: The classroom was really tidy when we were here. Wasn't it, Erin?

Erin: You could have eaten your dinner off the floor.

Lewis: Well, it was definitely a mess when I came in.

Yasmin: Lewis hasn't told us why **he** was in here.

Lewis: I came here to get my phone back. Mr Boyle took it, remember?

Yasmin: Yes, it was in his desk with the test papers.

Lewis: Well, there were no papers in the desk when I looked.

Yasmin: A likely story.

Myles: And what were you doing in the classroom, Yasmin?

Yasmin: Me? I always take my break in the classroom. The rest of you don't talk to me.

Erin: Because **you** don't talk to **us**!

Naomi: She thinks she's too good for us.

Yasmin: I don't think that!

Erin: You act like you do.

Ahmed: And you, Myles? What were you doing here?

Myles: Okay. I admit it. It was me.

Lewis: You stole the paper?

Myles: Me? No! I wrote the joke on the whiteboard.

Erin: That's supposed to be a joke?

Myles: Where's your sense of humour? That's a brilliant joke!

Yasmin: Well **I** don't think it's very funny, either.

Ahmed: Yeah, me neither. Anyway, there was no joke on the board when I came in.

Lewis: This isn't getting us anywhere.

Ahmed: I think it is. I think I can work it out.

Yasmin: You can?

Ahmed: Mr Boyle caught Erin and Naomi in here.

Naomi: And that's when he discovered the test paper was missing.

Erin: And the terrible joke was on the whiteboard.

Myles: It's a brilliant joke!

Lewis: That means you were in before the girls, Myles.

Why do bees hum?

Because they can't remember the words!

Myles: And when I came in, the classroom was really tidy.

Naomi: So you knew that Ahmed had been in.

Erin: We can always tell when Ahmed's been about.

Ahmed: And when I came in, there was no drawing on the board.

Myles: And when Lewis came in, the classroom was a mess.

Lewis: That's right.

Ahmed: And the paper was missing from the desk.

Erin: And the first person in the classroom was ...

All: Yasmin!

Yasmin: It wasn't me!

Lewis: So how did you know my phone was in the desk, then?

Pause.

Yasmin starts to cry.

Yasmin: I'm so ashamed!

Naomi: But why, Yasmin? You're really clever.

Erin: You didn't need to steal the paper.

Yasmin: I'm not clever. I just study really hard. And I didn't study for this test.

Myles: Who cares if you don't pass a test?

Yasmin: My mum and dad. They'd be really annoyed with me.

Ahmed: They'll be more annoyed that you stole the paper.

Yasmin: Now you'll all hate me even more.

Myles: Nobody hates you, Yasmin.

Ahmed: We always thought **you** didn't like **us**.

Yasmin: I do like you. I just don't think anybody likes me.

Erin: Don't cry, Yasmin.

Naomi: You'll have me crying, too.

Yasmin: I'm in so much trouble.

Lewis: Oh, okay. I'll say it was me.

Yasmin: You'd do that for me?

Lewis: I'm always in trouble anyway. And I just want to get out of here!

Yasmin: No, I'm going to confess. I don't deserve you being so nice to me.

Ahmed: I've got a better idea.

Erin: And what's that, Sherlock?

Ahmed: Well ... Hang on, what's that noise outside?

Myles: Sounds like footsteps.

Lewis: Mr Boyle's coming back!

Yasmin: Oh no! What am I going to do?

Erin: Don't worry, Yasmin.

Naomi: Yes, we'll sort it out – together.

Lost

Characters

Jacob — has a joke for all occasions

Maria — gets easily scared

Danny — likes to take charge

Kamran — always curious but doesn't always follow the rules

Ashti — likes to do the right thing

Lisa — always noticing things

All offstage calls and noises should be performed by the person playing Lisa.

Lisa: I don't know how, but somehow we've got lost!

Ashti: Miss Crane's going to be so cross with us.

Danny: We're not lost. I know exactly where we are. I've got the map.

Jacob: I think you've been reading it upside down.

Kamran: Miss Crane told us to stay where we were.

Danny: And of course you **always** obey the rules, don't you, Kamran?

Ashti: And you're always so bossy, Danny. Everybody has to do what you say!

Maria starts to look anxious.

Maria: Miss Crane will be looking for us, won't she?

Danny: Of course she will.

Offstage, a voice calls, "Maria!"

Maria: Did you hear that? It's Miss Crane. MISS CRANE! Over here!

Jacob: You **thought** you heard her before, Maria.

Ashti: That's how we got lost in the first place.

Danny: We're not lost! I've got the map.

Lisa: Well, we've been here before. I remember that tree!

Jacob: How can you tell that, Lisa? All trees look the same.

Lisa: No, the trunk on that one looks like a face.

Kamran: She's right. It does look like a face.

Danny: Rubbish.

Offstage, a voice calls, "Kamran!"

Kamran: Did you hear that? Miss Crane! We're here!

Kamran runs towards the voice.

Maria: Come back, Kamran! We'll get lost again.

Lisa: We should just stay here.

Ashti: No, we have to go with Kamran now. We shouldn't split up.

Danny: Okay, but stick with me. Remember ...

Maria: We know. You've got the map.

They run to catch up with Kamran.

Ashti: Did you see her, Kamran?

Kamran: No, but I definitely heard her.

Maria: Why do we keep hearing her, and never seeing her?

Jacob uses a spooky voice.

Jacob: Getting scared, Maria?

Maria: It's getting dark. I want to go home.

Ashti: Try your phone again, Danny.

Danny: There's no reception. I keep trying it.

Offstage, an owl hoots.

Maria: What was that?

Lisa: It was only Jacob, trying to be funny. Stop it, Jacob.

Jacob: Oh, come on. Who wants to hear a scary story?

Maria: Not me!

Jacob: Have you heard the one about the pupils who got lost on a school trip?

Maria interrupts Jacob.

Maria: ▶ Hey look! There are people over there.
(She shouts.)
Hey!

Ashti: ▶ I think it's Miss Crane and the rest of the class – I can't quite see …

All:	Miss Crane! Over here!
Jacob:	They didn't hear us.
Kamran:	They didn't even see us.
Ashti:	Come on, we'll go after them.

They run in the direction of the voices.

Ashti: Where did they go?

Maria: How could we lose them?

Lisa: This is all your fault, Danny.

Danny: My fault!

Jacob mimics Danny.

Jacob: "I've got the map," you said. "I won't get you lost," you said! Ha!

Danny: You didn't have to come with me.

Offstage, the wind howls eerily.

Maria: What was that?

Ashti: Stop that, Jacob.

Jacob: That wasn't me. Honest.

Lisa: Who was it, then?

Kamran: We're in the woods. It could be an animal.

Maria: An animal! Like a wolf?

Ashti: No, of course not. He means ... like a squirrel.

Jacob: Yeah ... that sounded just like a squirrel **howling**.

Maria: Why didn't Miss Crane and the rest of the class see us?

Danny: If it **was** Miss Crane.

Maria: Of course it was Miss Crane.

Ashti: I wish we could find her.

Jacob: Maybe she's lost as well.

Danny: We are **not** lost!

Lisa: We know. You've got the map.

Danny: Yes, I've got the ... Oh no!

Kamran: "Oh no" ... what?

Danny: I've lost the map. It was in my pocket and now ...

Kamran: It's gone?

Danny: It must have fallen out of my pocket when we were running.

Offstage, a voice calls, "Jacob!"

Jacob: Did you hear that? It was Miss Crane.

Lisa: I never heard anything.

Ashti: It came from over there ...
Miss Crane! We're here!

Danny: Are you sure it was her?

Kamran: There's something funny going on.

Jacob: I really did hear her. I wasn't trying
to be funny, not this time.

Maria: He doesn't mean that kind of funny,
do you, Kamran?

Lisa: Oh no – we're back to where we started. Look, there's that tree again.

Jacob: How can you tell that, Lisa? All trees look the same.

Ashti: It's not the same tree.

Lisa: It looks like there's a face on the trunk of that one.

Kamran: You said that before, Lisa.

Lisa: No, I didn't.

Ashti: Miss Crane's going to be so cross with us.

Kamran: You said that before too, Ashti.

Jacob: Let's face it. We're lost.

Danny: We are not lost. I've got the map.

Kamran: You said you lost it.

Danny: No, it was in my pocket all the time.

Kamran: You said it fell out of your pocket.

Jacob: I didn't hear him say that.

Kamran: This is what I mean about "something funny". We keep going round in circles.

Maria: You're scaring me.

Ashti: Don't listen to him, Maria.

Kamran: I was beginning to think …

Danny: Think what?

Kamran: We saw Miss Crane and the rest of the class, but they didn't see us …

Lisa: Or hear us …

Kamran: It's almost as if …

Jacob: As if we were … lost?
Oh, come on, Kamran.

Lisa: I wish we hadn't got lost …

Pause.

Maria is suddenly really excited.

Maria: There's Miss Crane! I can see her!

Danny: There's nobody there, Maria.

Jacob: No, she's right – I see her too!

Lisa sounds relieved.

Lisa: So do I. MISS CRANE!

Ashti: Everything's okay.

Danny: For a minute there you were freaking us all out, Kamran.

Jacob: But everything's fine now. There's Miss Crane.

Lisa: She's found us.

Jacob: Come on, Kamran!

Maria: It's all right now ...
(She pauses.)
... isn't it, Kamran?

Kamran: Yes, it's all right now ... I hope ...